SUPER BUS 2

María José Lobo ◆ **Pepita Subirà**

Course consultant: **Sagrario Salaberri**

Pupil's Book

Introduction page 2

1 The Circus

page 3

2 Food

page 9

3 My Town

page 15

4 It's cold

page 21

5 What time is it?

page 27

6 Wild Animals

page 33

7 End of School Year

page 39

Halloween activities page 45 ◆ **Christmas activities** page 46
Carnival activities page 48

1 Listen and point 📼

My name's Steve.

I'm Kate.

My name's Alex.

My name's Mr Magico.

I'm Alison.

MAGIC CASE

2 Song 🎵

I want to go to school
Get on the bus!
Get on the bus!

I want to play a game
Get on the bus!
Get on the bus!

I want to sing a song
Get on the bus!
Get on the bus!

GET ON SUPER BUS!

BUS STOP

1

THE CIRCUS

1 Listen and play

2 Listen and point

juggler

acrobat

clown

magician

3 Mr Magico's trick   Cut out 1 Activity Book page 59

What number is it?

Twenty.

Circus Tricks

1 Listen and say 🔲   Spot two mistakes.

The Golden Circus

elephants

tigers

lions

horses

magician

clowns

monkeys

jugglers

acrobats

Saturday 15th October, Sunday 16th October
Tickets: Adults £10, children £6

2 Listen and do 🔲

3 Song 🎵

THE GOLDEN CIRCUS

We're at The Golden Circus
What a lot of fun!

Look at the tigers and the monkeys
And the elephants too!
Look at the lions and the horses
Lots of things to see and do!

We're at The Golden Circus
What a lot of fun!

Look at the acrobats and
  the juggler
And look at the clown!
He's very funny
With his trousers
  falling down!

4 Listen and repeat 📼

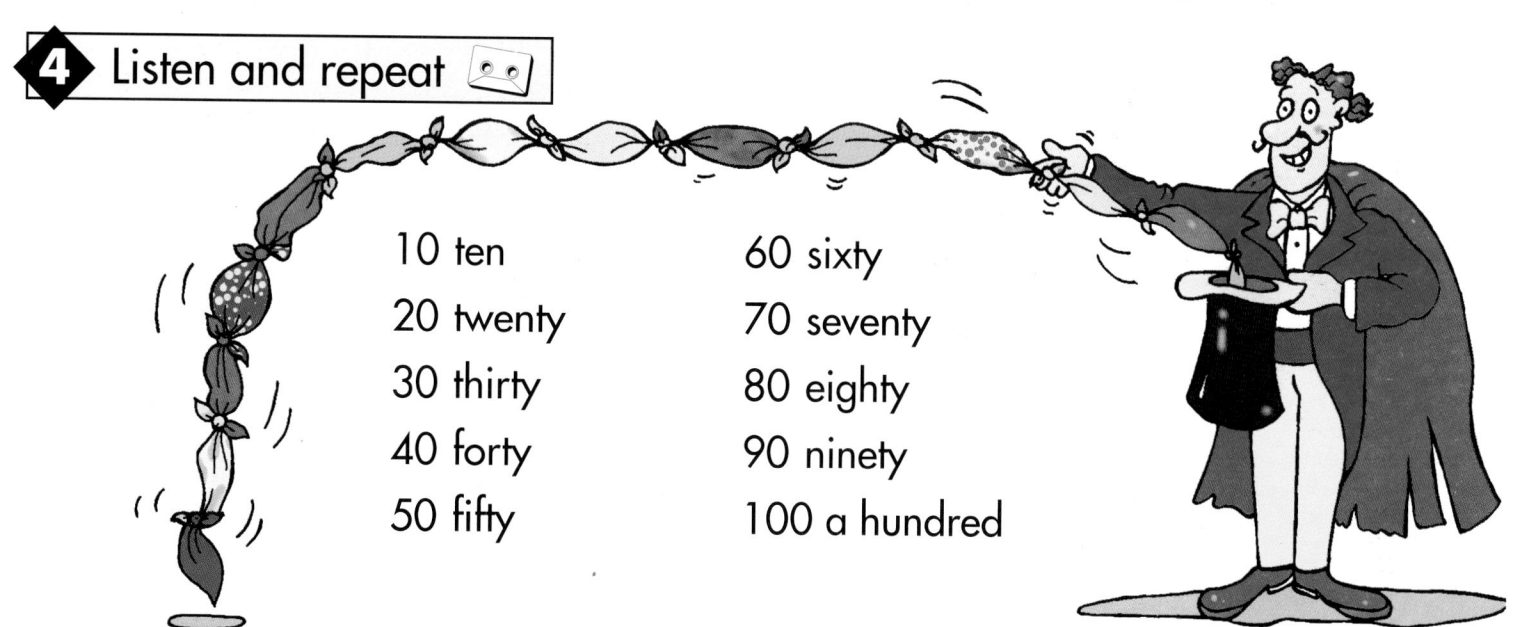

10 ten	60 sixty
20 twenty	70 seventy
30 thirty	80 eighty
40 forty	90 ninety
50 fifty	100 a hundred

Twelve months in a year
Twelve months, twelve months

January, February, March
April, May
June, July
August, September
October, November
December comes at last

2 FOOD

1 Listen and point

milk shake

sweets

lollipops

cola

ham

fish

oranges

grapes

bananas

apples

2 Game — Can you say ...?

3 Speak

I like ...

I don't like ...

What's for dinner today?

Listen and look

1 Chant

Do you like apples?
Yes, I do. Yes, I do.
I like apples.
I love apples! Mmmmmm!

Do you like fish?
No, I don't. No, I don't.
I don't like fish.
I hate fish. YUCK!

2 Make food cards

Cut out 2 Activity Book page 61

You need: crayons

1 cut out

2 colour

3 match

apples

sweets

sausages

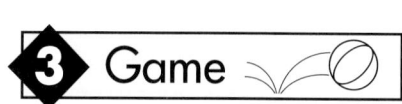

3 Game

4 Listen, point and say

breakfast

lunch

dinner

5 Mr Magico's trick

   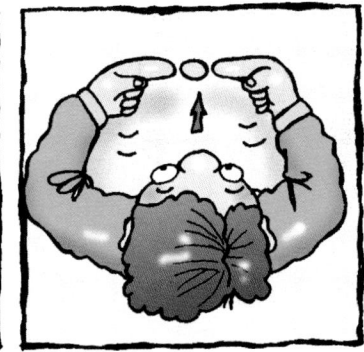

1 Join the index fingers.

2 Put the fingers in front of your eyes.

3 Move your fingers near your eyes.

4 Move your fingers away from your eyes.

6 Chant

Coffee, coffee
Cake and biscuits
Cake and biscuits
Fish and chips
Fish and chips
Soup!

7 Act out

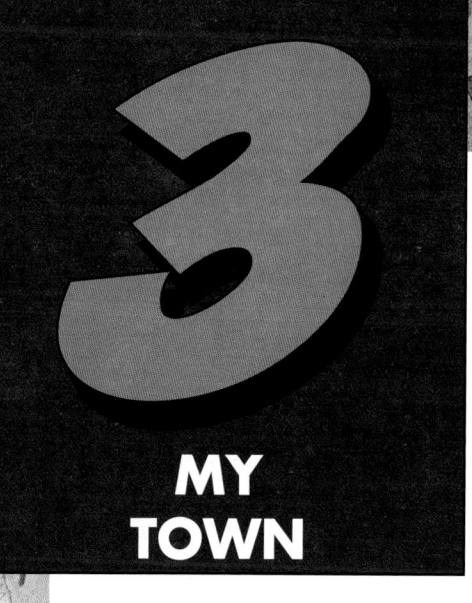

3 MY TOWN

1 Look and speak

What does it mean?

1

2

3

2 Moving game

Listen and do.

3 Song

A B C D E F G
H I J K L M
N O P Q R S T U
V W X Y Z

THE MYSTERIOUS MAN

Listen and look 📼

① SCHOOL

② PARK STREET

③ SUPERMARKET

④ PET SHOP

1 Song

Rat-a-tat-tat, rat-a-tat-tat
That's the way the postman knocks
Rat-a-tat-tat, rat-a-tat-tat
Everyday at eight o'clock
One letter, two letters, three letters, four
Rat-a-tat-tat, rat-a-tat-tat
That's the way the postman knocks
at the door

2 Make an envelope

You need: paper glue

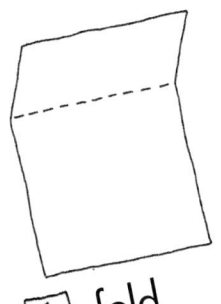

1 fold

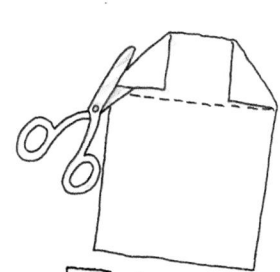

2 fold and cut

3 fold and glue

4 write

3 Game

Who lives at 14 Park Street?

Alison Jones
14 Park St.
Oxford

4 Write

Stand up and open the window.

Jump.

Touch Maria's head.

5 Listen and point

SUPERMARKET   PET SHOP

1   2

SWEET SHOP   Clothes Shop   BOOK SHOP   TOY SHOP

3   4   5   6

6 Pairs game A

What's missing?

BOOK SHOP 1

PET SHOP 9

SUPERMARKET 5

SWEET SHOP 14

PARK STREET

ELM STREET

RIVER STREET

A   Where's the …?
B   It's at …

police station
toy shop
clothes shop

6 Pairs game B — What's missing?

supermarket
book shop
pet shop
sweet shop

B Where's the ...?
A It's at ...

8 Make a shop ✂

Cut out 3 Activity Book page 63

You need:  crayons  glue

7 Mr Magico's trick ✍ ✨

Write a number 1–30.
Subtract 2.
Multipy this number by 3.
Add 12.
Divide this number by 3.
Add 5.
Subtract your number.
Abracadabra!
You've got number 7.

| 1 | draw and colour | 2 |  write |

 draw and colour

 write

3 cut out

4  fold

5 glue

6  glue

4
IT'S COLD

1 Listen and point

jumper

anorak

scarf

gloves

2 Game

It's hot.

It's cold.

3 Listen and play

T-shirt.

BALLOON RIDE

Listen and look

1 Chant

A scarf for winter
A cap for spring
A dress for summer
A coat for me
To wear in autumn
How can it be?
It's cold!
Can't you see?

2 Listen and repeat

The 1st of February.

The 2nd of February.

FEBRUARY

1 2 3 4
5 6 7 8 9 10 11
12 13 14 15 16 17 18
19 20 21 22 23 24 25
26 27 28

The 3rd of February.

The 7th of February.

The 9th of February.

3 Game

I'm going on a balloon ride and I'm taking ...

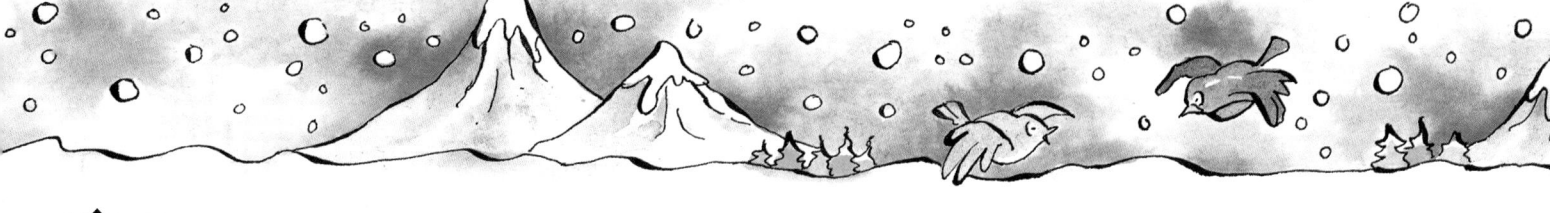

 4 Song 🎵

When I go up in the air
in my big big balloon
my friends look up and shout
'Hi! Are you going to the moon?'

When I go up in the air
I look down down down
I can only say 'Goodbye!'
And go into the clouds

5 Mr Magico's trick

Put your hands like this.

Pull his hands apart.

The trick!

6 Game

Tennis!

7 Balloon race   Cut out 4 Activity Book page 65

You need: crayons

5

WHAT TIME IS IT?

1 Moving game
Listen and do.

2 Listen and point

1 It's one o'clock.

2 It's seven o'clock.

3 It's a quarter past one.

4 It's a quarter past seven.

5 It's half past one.

6 It's half past seven.

7 It's a quarter to two.

8 It's a quarter to eight.

1 Read and match

TV PROGRAMMES
SATURDAY EVENING

1 **5:00**
CARTOON
Superduck

2 **5:15**
NEWS

3 **5:30**
SPORTS
Basketball

4 **6:00**
NATURE
Elephants

5 **6:45**
MUSIC
The Top Ten

6 **7:00**
HORROR FILM
Dracula

a
A quarter past five

b
Half past five

c
A quarter to seven

d
Six o'clock

e
Five o'clock

f
Seven o'clock

2 Mr Magico's trick

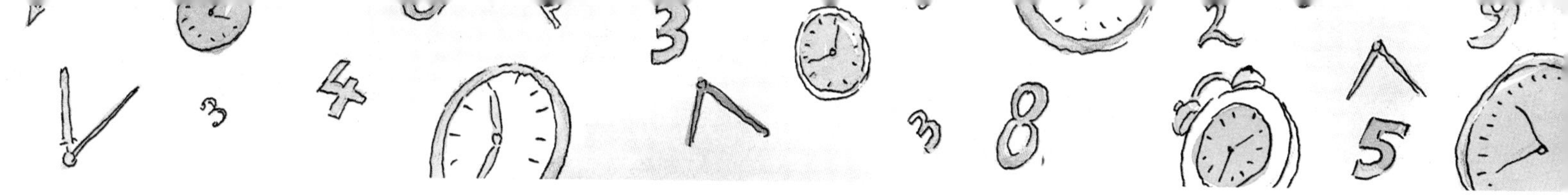

3 Chant

It's time to watch TV!
What's on today. Let's see.
A cartoon. Oh, good!
The News. Okay.
A nature programme. Wow!
The music show. Hurray!
A film at 10. Fantastic! Great!
Oh, no! Too late! It's time to go to bed.

4 Match and play Cut out 5 Activity Book page 67

You need:  glue

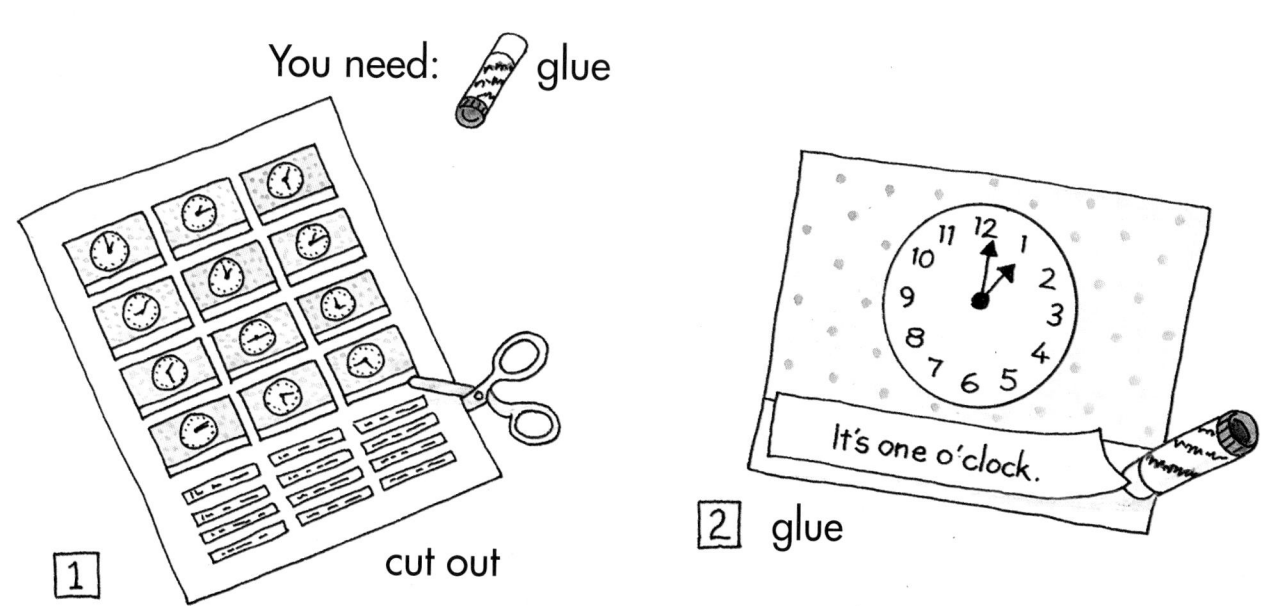

1 cut out

2 glue

It's one o'clock.

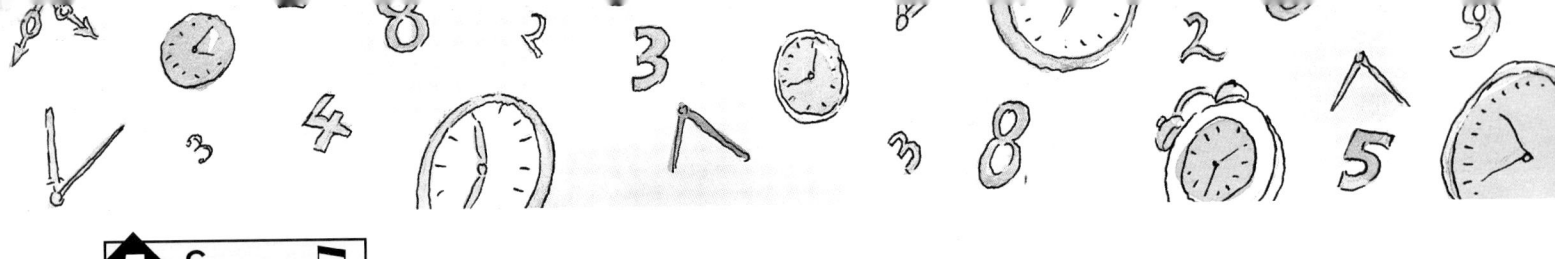

5 Song ♫

What day is it?
Ahh! It's Sunday
Time to rest and time to play
There's no school today

What day is it?
It's Monday
Quick, get up and catch the bus
Don't be late for school

6 Interview

Choose six questions.

What's your name?
How old are you?
Where do you live?
What time do you get up?
What time do you have breakfast?
What time do you go to school?
What's your favourite colour?
What's your favourite number?
What's your favourite TV programme?
Do you like sports?
What's your favourite sport?
What's your favourite food?

6

WILD ANIMALS

| elephant | lion | eagle | giraffe | hippo |

2 Moving game Listen and point.

| 1 | 2 | 3 | 4 | 5 | 6 |

WHY GIRAFFES HAVE LONG NECKS

Listen and look 📼

1 **O**nce upon a time there was a young giraffe.

2 Mr Elephant, can you catch the moon? She eats my leaves.

3 Mr Lion, can you catch the moon? She eats my leaves.

4 Miss Eagle, can you catch the moon? She eats my leaves.

1 Listen and read 🔘

Elephants are very big animals. They've got big ears and a very long trunk. They are grey. Elephants live in grasslands and eat grass, leaves and fruit.

Giraffes are very tall animals. They are brown and yellow. They've got long legs and a very long neck. Giraffes live in grasslands and eat leaves.

Lions are strong animals. They are yellow. They've got big teeth and a long tail. Lions live in grasslands and eat animals.

Hippos are very big animals. They are grey. They've got a big mouth, short legs and small ears. Hippos live in lakes and rivers and eat grass.

2 Act out 🎭 🔘

Act out the story.

3 Point to the objects you collect

stamps

toy cars

coins

picture cards

postcards

stickers

4 Listen and count

100	200	300	400
a hundred	two hundred	three hundred	four hundred

500	600	700
five hundred	six hundred	seven hundred

800	900	1000
eight hundred	nine hundred	a thousand

5 Song 🎵

When I go to the zoo
Go to the zoo
I see lions and tigers
And big elephants
I see hippos and camels
And hungry crocodiles

When I go to the zoo
Go to the zoo
I see bears and penguins
And monkeys swinging by
I see zebras and giraffes
And eagles flying high

6 Make a zoo ✂

Cut out 6 Activity Book page 69

You need: crayons   glue

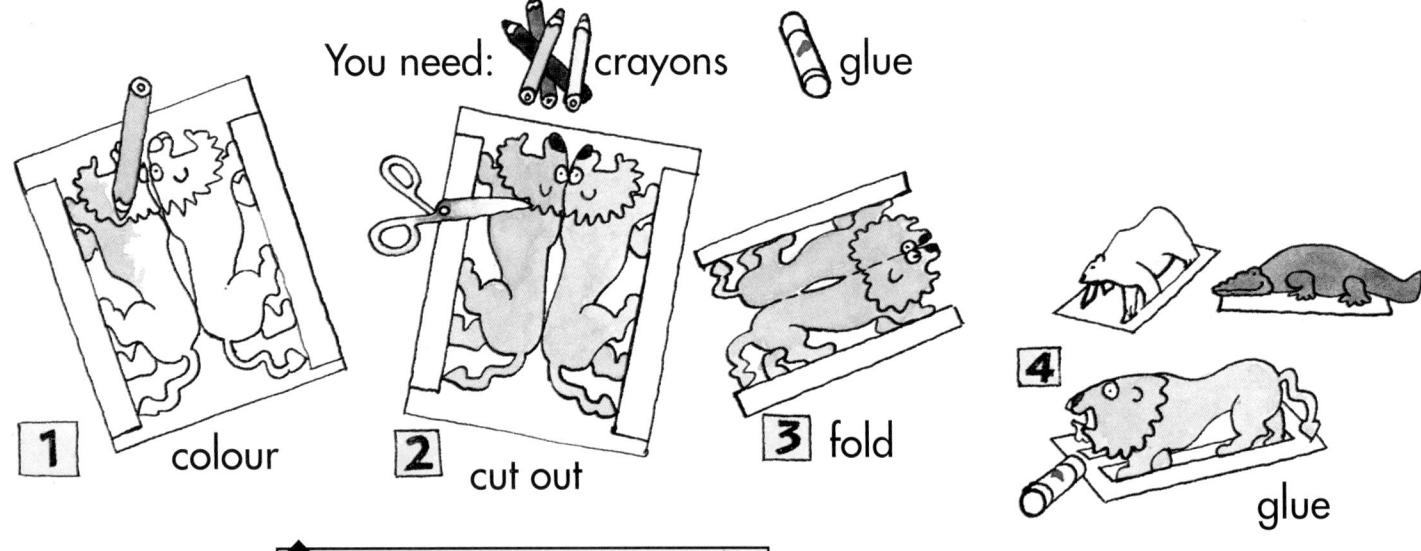

1 colour

2 cut out

3 fold

4

glue

7 Mr Magico's trick

   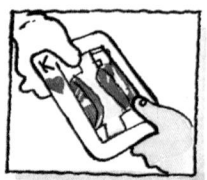  

Count the cards.

Hold this card.

Show it to the children.

Give me the card.

Count the cards.

The card has disappeared.

7
END OF SCHOOL YEAR

1 Listen and match 📼

1 Woof! Woof!

2

Miaow! Miaow!

3

Squeak! Squeak!

4

Quack! Quack!

5

Hee-haw! Hee-haw!

Cock-a-doodle-doo!

6

2 Speak | Can you …?

1

2

3

4

5

6

| high jump | play basketball | swim | skateboard | run | play football |

Pretty Ritty

Listen and look

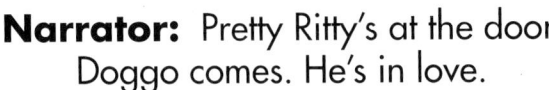

Narrator: Pretty Ritty's at the door. Doggo comes. He's in love.

Doggo: Pretty Ritty, marry me.

Pretty Ritty: Well, well. Let me see. Can you sing a song for me?

Doggo: Yes. Listen. Woof! Woof! Woof! Woof!

Pretty Ritty: Oh, no! I don't like your voice!

Narrator: Poor Doggo. Off he goes. Pretty Ritty's at the door. Donko comes. He's in love.

Donko: Pretty Ritty, marry me.

Pretty Ritty: Well, well. Let me see. Can you sing a song for me?

Donko: Yes. Listen. Hee-haw! Hee-haw! Hee-haw! Hee-haw!

Pretty Ritty: Oh, no! I don't like your voice!

Narrator: Poor Donko. Off he goes. Pretty Ritty's at the door. Cocko comes. He's in love.

Cocko: Pretty Ritty, marry me.

Pretty Ritty: Well, well. Let me see.
Can you sing a song for me?

Cocko: Yes. Listen. Cock-a-doodle-doo!
Cock-a-doodle-doo!

Pretty Ritty: Oh, no! I don't like
your voice!

Narrator: Poor Cocko. Off he goes.
Pretty Ritty's at the door.
Catto comes. He's not in love.

Catto: Pretty Ritty, marry me.

Pretty Ritty: Well, well. Let me see.
Can you sing a song for me?

Catto: Yes. Listen. Miaow! Miaow!
Miaow! Miaow!

Pretty Ritty: I like your voice.
Yes. I'll marry you.

Narrator: But Catto's hungry. Mmmmm!
He's a cat.
Ritty's there.
She's a rat.

Catto: Mmmmm!

Narrator: Off he jumps!
And off she runs!

Pretty Ritty: I like your voice, but you are
bad. HEEEEEELP!!!

1 Match

1 Catto's a …   **2** Donko's a …   **3** Cocko's a …   **4** Doggo's a …   **5** Pretty Ritty's a …

| cock   cat   dog   rat   donkey |

2 Match

1

2

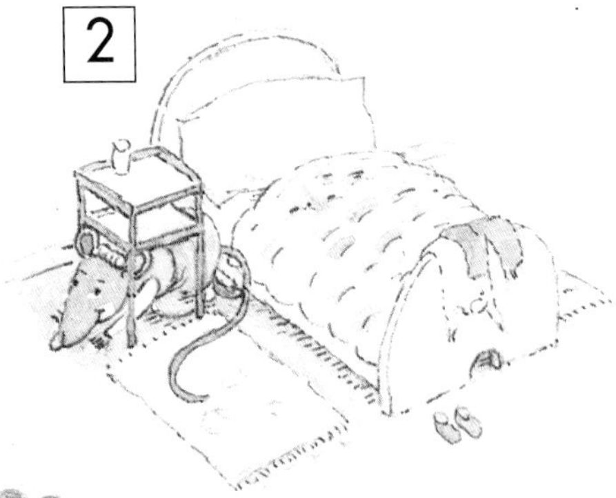

3

4

5

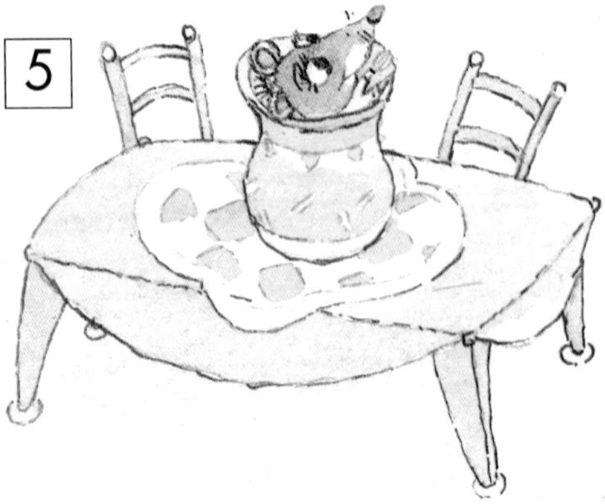

| behind the sofa   under the table   in the vase   on the fridge   at the door |

3 Make a mask ✂ Cut out 7 Activity Book page 71

You need: 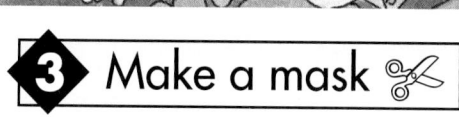 crayons   an elastic band

1 cut out

2 draw and colour

3 fix the elastic band

4 Act out 😮 Act out the play.

5 Song ♫

The leaves are growing. It's spring!
Open the window. It's warm outside!

The sun is shining. It's summer!
Put on your hat. It's hot outside!

The leaves are falling. It's autumn!
Close the window. It's cool outside!

Snow is falling. It's winter!
Read by the fire. It's cold outside!

6 Mr Magico's trick

1

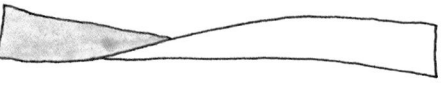
2 Twist the paper.

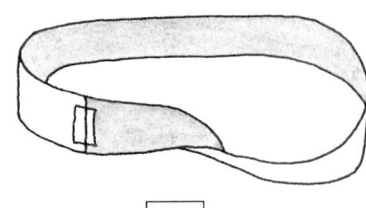
3 Join the ends.

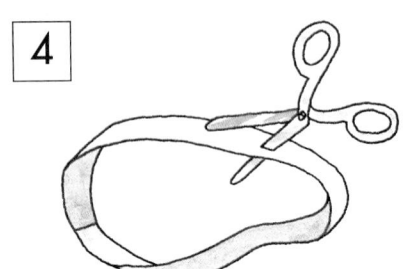
4 Make a hole
in the middle.

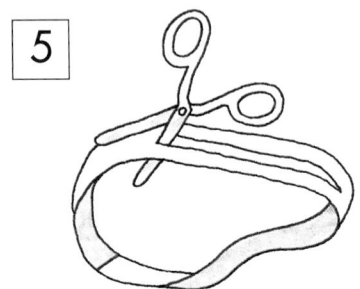
5 Cut along the middle.

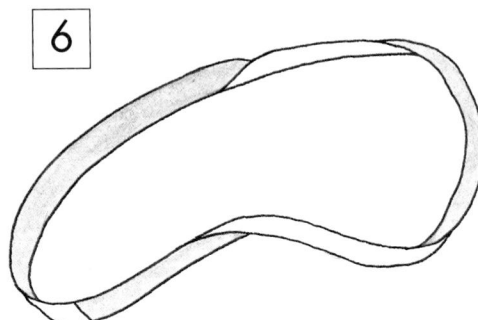
6 The circle is very big.

7 Song

Spring has gone
Summer's here
It's now the end
Of the school year

Goodbye to our teacher
Goodbye to our class
Goodbye everyone
Goodbye Super Bus!

HALLOWEEN

It's 31st October. Look at the sky.
The moon is in the sky.
The children are celebrating
Halloween. At the windows
there are pumpkins with a candle
inside.
The children are wearing masks
and costumes.

They are in the street. They are
playing tricks.

I'm a ghost. WOO!
I'm a witch. CACKLE!
I'm a skeleton. RATTLE!
I'm a black cat. MIAOWWWW!
I'm Dracula. HEE! HEE! HEE!

2 Song ♪♫

Girls and boys
Go out to play
The moon is bright
On Halloween night

Take your candle
Take your mask
The moon is bright
On Halloween night

Look for witches
Look for ghosts
The moon is bright
On Halloween night

Abracadabra wizzy woo
I want to play with you

CHRISTMAS

1 Song ♪♫

O Christmas tree, O Christmas tree
How lovely are your branches
O Christmas tree, O Christmas tree
How lovely are your branches
In beauty green they'll always grow
Through summer sun and winter snow
O Christmas tree, O Christmas tree
How lovely are your branches

CARNIVAL

1 Make a carnival mask ✂ Cut out 10 Activity Book page 77

You need: crayons   coloured paper   glue   elastic band

ribbons

wool

1 cut out

3
fix the elastic band

2
colour and glue

2 Song ♫

Come and dance
Come and play
It's ... CARNIVAL!

Hurry up
Join us
It's ... CARNIVAL!

Oh what fun
Let's laugh and play
It's ... CARNIVAL!

Hurry up
Join us
It's ... CARNIVAL!